D1387876

JEREMY GUSCOTT

A PICTORIAL TRIBUTE

INTRODUCTION BY
STEPHEN JONES

PHOTOGRAPHS BY
ALLSPORT UK
COLORSPORT   **SPEDEGRAFIX 99**

Queen Anne Press

A QUEEN ANNE PRESS BOOK

© Lennard Associates Limited 2000

First published in 2000 by
Queen Anne Press, a division of
Lennard Associates Limited
Mackerye End
Harpenden, Herts AL5 5DR

A catalogue entry is available from the British Library

ISBN (hardback - jacketed) 1 85291 635 4
ISBN (hardback - laminated boards) 1 85291 634 6

Production Editor: Chris Marshall
Cover Design/Design Consultant: Paul Cooper
Reproduction: Prism Digital

Printed and bound in Great Britain by
Butler & Tanner, Frome and London

Jeremy Guscott

Bath, England and
the British Lions

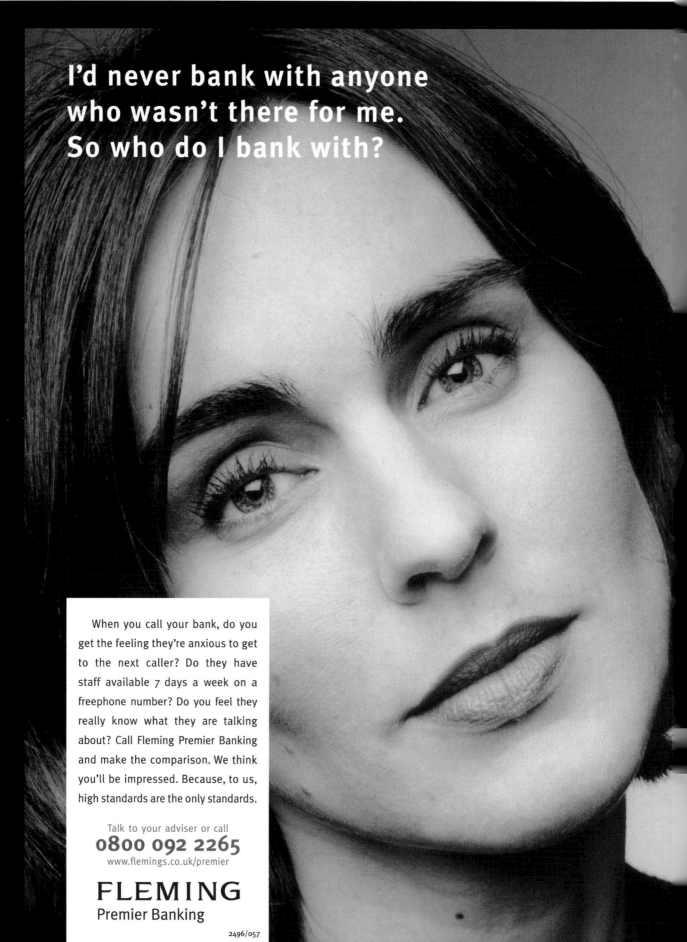

I'd never bank with anyone who wasn't there for me. So who do I bank with?

When you call your bank, do you get the feeling they're anxious to get to the next caller? Do they have staff available 7 days a week on a freephone number? Do you feel they really know what they are talking about? Call Fleming Premier Banking and make the comparison. We think you'll be impressed. Because, to us, high standards are the only standards.

Talk to your adviser or call
0800 092 2265
www.flemings.co.uk/premier

FLEMING
Premier Banking

2496/057

Contents

I'd never bank with anyone who didn't make me feel valued. So who do I bank with?

Next time you speak to your bank, try asking for more than the balance of your account. Ask them to do something out of the ordinary, something they wouldn't normally do, except for their most valued clients. Ask them to go the extra mile. If they do, fine. If they don't, try this. Call Fleming Premier Banking. You'll find that, with us, extraordinary service comes as standard.

Talk to your adviser or call

0800 092 2265

www.flemings.co.uk/premier

FLEMING
Premier Banking

2496/057

Foreword

I am delighted that Fleming Premier Banking is sponsoring this pictorial tribute to Jeremy Guscott, surely one of the finest English rugby players of all time.

As well as representing his home town of Bath with distinction and considerable success, Jerry has brought his great talent to the international arena with the England team and, of course, as a key member of three British Lions squads.

Style, skill, competitiveness and strength are attributes you would readily associate with Jerry Guscott. Indeed they are vital ingredients for success at the highest levels of any sport today. They are also the qualities needed for success in business, not least in the fiercely competitive world of financial services. This is the arena in which Fleming Premier Banking operates.

Fleming Premier Banking, as the name implies, is part of the Flemings group of companies. And we occupy a unique position in the 'premier banking' marketplace. Our long history is complemented by a modern, progressive outlook and a resourceful, pioneering spirit. For example, Fleming Premier Banking was the innovator of telephone-based, branchless banking. Today we offer a highly competitive range of current and savings accounts for individuals, businesses, charities, clubs and other organisations.

Finally, I do hope you will enjoy the contents of this fine book, which I am sure will last as a richly-deserved tribute to a truly special player.

Piers A. White.

Retail Banking Director
Fleming Premier Banking

Introduction

by Stephen Jones
of The Sunday Times

I t was one of the most frightening moments of my journalistic career. I was sitting in the front room of Jeremy Guscott's former home in Bath, just above the A4 on the road into the city. The occasion was the first session as we conspired on his autobiography, and the intention was to tape his thoughts on aspects of his career for me to knock into shape for the book, *At the Centre*. He is unquestionably the greatest back ever produced in England, but one opinion, however widely it is held, can't make a whole book. I needed more.

As it was the first session and we didn't know each other that well, I decided that we'd start with something fresh in the memory. His early life and background, his often-problematical early years, his start in mini-rugby, his arrival as part of Bath's glorious march, his advent as an England player and British Lion – all these we could leave until a later date when we were in the swim of things. As it was only a few weeks since the 1993 Lions tour of New Zealand had ended, I suggested we start there.

'Right,' I said. 'What do you remember about the 2nd Test in Wellington? Let's have your thoughts.' This was the (memorable) Test where the Lions hammered the All Blacks and squared the series. There was a long silence, broken only by my tape machine as it whirred gently in the background.

'Hang on. That Test was in Christchurch, wasn't it?' said the Memory Man, eventually. It was a grim thought that we were contracted to provide 100,000 words on the life and sporting career of an admittedly vivid subject and he couldn't remember something that had happened a few weeks before. I then decided to investigate his family background. 'Got any really interesting relatives?' I asked. 'Naw, not really,' he said. It was only much later than I learned that one of his relatives had been one of the most dashing, brilliant and famous spies that Britain's secret service ever had, a man who had operated undercover in Bolshevik Russia and in parts of the Far East, was wrongly implicated in the murder of a group called the Baku Commissars and spent much of the rest of his life in Britain living under an assumed name because Russian death squads were after him. It was only near his death that his secret and his real identity were revealed.

Good old Jerry. No-one interesting in your family, then.

I was not to know then that not only would his memory prove reasonably secure when we were over the initial hurdles but also that I would find the experience not only as difficult as is the normal lot of the ghostwriter but also one of the most rewarding. In common with the rest of the world, I had always been fascinated by Guscott. Not only electrified by his play, but also intrigued by his character. When he asked me to work with him on the book project, I was not only proud ('Jerry's begged me to do his book. I'm thinking about it. Maybe I can fit it in.') but also intrigued.

Was the real Guscott the man prone to sudden and devastating put-downs, but was that the ghost of an ironic smile on his face as he delivered them? Was he an arrogant, er... twit? Was he really as cool as his demeanour suggested, and as sartorially sharp that he was once runner-up to Terence Stamp in some magazine's best-dressed man competition? Was he some West Country equivalent of Ralph in *Lord of the Flies*, who became popular not because he noisily buzzed round with the rest but because of his stillness? Was he the man of such arrogance and self-confidence that he did indeed, as Richard Hill insists, reply to a girl who had asked him to dance by saying: 'Why, is it Halloween yet?' (To be fair, he strongly denies it!)

Or was the real Jeremy the guy who'd come over when no-one else was around and be charming, funny, modest and interested in what you were doing? (I know a writer who spent six months ghostwriting a book and the subject never once asked the author about his family, or if he even had one.) Was he the man who would make friends in every team for whom he played and had a network of contacts around the rugby world, but who would be happiest spending time with his mates from the old days in Bath, Peter Blackett and Chalkie Wardle? To be frank, I used to find it as unnerving when Jeremy came up being nice as it was when he delivered some devastating mickey-take that left you spluttering for a rejoinder.

Perhaps another aspect of the same question was this. Was the real Jeremy more like Henry, his gracious, charming and understated father, or Sue, his ebullient mother, who once enlivened a Bath Rugby Supporters' evening, which I attended as one of the panel, by reading out predictions I had made in *The Sunday Times* over the years which had come horrendously unstuck? Once people realised that I was conspiring with Guscott on a book, other people started asking me the question I was trying to answer for myself. 'What's he really like?'

The answer is that he is one of the best and most genuine guys I have met in rugby, and in a sport where you can count the people you don't like on the fingers of one hand, then perhaps it might be considered a recommendation. It seems to me that his success lies in the fact that he has struck a happy medium. He is, indeed, the most devastating deliverer of one-line crushers, well able to hold his own in the almost violently sharp verbalising of the Bath dressing room. You might say that he can be sharp with people who try to barge into his company, but on the other hand, you can believe, as I firmly do, that considering the number of people who want a piece of him in every environment in which he finds himself, then his patience is remarkable. I've been with him when a ceaseless stream of people have come up wanting autographs, or to be photographed with him or to tell him how well, or badly, he's playing. He usually manages it wonderfully well. When he was (wrongly) accused of assaulting a pedestrian in Bath, I and all those who knew him well said that it did not sound at all like the Jerry we knew, and in his exoneration was the evidence that bore out our thoughts.

He has a star quality which is undeniable, which has appealed to companies and television producers in droves. He is, as those people who deal professionally with him will swear, a consummate professional. If he says he will meet you for lunch or some kind of assignment at a specific time he will be there a minute early. He is successful as a television personality, has transcended the sports field entirely by appearing on *Gladiators*. He once tried to convince me that he was uncomfortable sitting in the front row of the programme *An Audience with the Bee Gees*, one of those luvvie spectaculars. 'I didn't want to go, but Jayne [his wife] likes the Bee Gees. They wanted me to ask a question too, but there was no way. I got Rory [Underwood] to do it.'

But the essential Guscott is also a down-home West Country bloke. The guy on TV and in the ad campaigns and personal appearances is a man doing a job, not the man himself. Even if there are few people around these days who remember being picked up by Guscott in his days as a driver with the Badgerline bus company (apart from about 3,000 people in The Shed at Gloucester, who always used to remind him), then it is true that his local roots are profoundly deep and his identification with Bath is not only deep but inviolable. He had offers from all kinds of clubs in rugby union and rugby league in both hemispheres, but it was a major consideration that he did not wish to leave Bath. Especially not for the bright lights of London, where the uninitiated would believe him to be most at home.

It became blindingly obvious as I grew to know him a little better that his family means infinitely more than all 65 of his England caps, all his British Lions glories and all his TV appearances lumped together. If there is a more significant noise on interview tapes I have made with him over the years than the whirring as he marshals his memory, then it is of the thunderously noisy interruptions caused by the tumultuous entry of Imogen, Holly and Saskia, his daughters. For about 20 minutes, until Guscott can persuade them to play in another room, the tape is full of shrieks and crashes and protestations of the warmest of family groups. Jayne Guscott is still actively considering forgiving her husband for picking her up for their first date, years ago at Bath railway station, in a filthy yellow van from his days as a manual worker in the West Country. She can usually manage to radiate a serenity entirely out of keeping with the maelstrom. It is not an unusual thing, of course, for young men to claim that their life changed, and old anxieties were made ludicrous, by the arrival of their baby daughters (or sons), but in Guscott's case, he felt the emotion with a particular sharpness.

The stories of his early life have become familiar to me not just because we examined them in the book – although one in particular, the Gareth Chilcott assessment of the opposition, has become a standing joke between us. Chilcott once impressed the young Guscott no end at a team meeting when he was asked to assess the opposition for that Saturday. Coochie went through the team with some wisdom and ended with a ringing warning. 'They're big, strong and robust,' he said. Guscott was less impressed when Chilcott concluded the next 147 assessments of the opposition over the years with the view that they were 'big, strong and robust'. Bath, apparently, met so many teams that were big, strong and robust that it was a wonder than any of their squad were still alive to tell the tales.

But other stories gained wider exposure, and have become endlessly recycled in a host of profile articles. The one that has become most famous of all is obviously Tricky's Training Trip. This came early in Guscott's career as a senior at Bath. He had emerged from a rather chippy, chirpy early life that included expulsion from Ralph Allen School after a string of misdemeanours culminating in abuse of a football referee in an inter-school match, his estrangement from Henry, his father, which caused him to move out of the family home in his teens and to return long months later, and a search for a fitting post through a fair few different jobs – in supermarkets, bricklaying and bus-driving.

The idea that he was becoming slightly more rounded as a personality, however, was not one shared by some of his colleagues at Bath, where he was already an embryo sensation and on the verge of first-team action. The details of what happened on Trick's Trip are agreed by both parties in all respects, bar the make of the car involved, since they both insist that it was different to the other's recollection. But not in dispute is the fact that Guscott arrived at the Recreation Ground for training, found that it was postponed and was now to be held at Lambridge, a few miles away along the A4. David Trick, the Bath and England wing, a famously easy-going and popular character, offered Guscott a lift. The idea that people might not like him bothered Guscott more than he cared to admit at the time, so when he ascertained from Trick that he was regarded as a big-headed and mouthy so-and-so, a pain in the backside, it took him aback more than any tackle. 'I thought that if Tricky was saying that, then what were the others saying?' It was a signpost along the road to a greater maturity, to a time where Guscott retained all the self-confidences conveyed by a glorious talent, retained what might be termed a beneficial sporting arrogance, but lost the wasteful arrogance off the field which had caused the patient Trick to say his piece.

Guscott has never lost that singularity, he has always been a man apart, affecting an aloofness; once famously claiming never to be bored by the interminable number of speeches in an interminable number of team meetings, because he never listened anyway. He never cultivated quite the aloofness of a David Campese, who could be away playing with the ball by himself as the Australians lined up for the national anthem. With Guscott, it was more tongue-in-cheek gestures, living up to people's mistaken perceptions to keep them guessing; something that revealed an irreverence and sense of humour rather than a true self-centredness.

It was a balance that was difficult to achieve, and the fact that Guscott managed it so well is a considerable tribute. Perhaps he never became so influential a senior player as he might have been, although he has advised the likes of Matt Perry and Mike Tindall and the other young Bath backs of late. But he became – this man who cultivated the air of an outsider – a true team man. He may have been a classy back, but it is probably significant that among his closest friends on the England scene have been the hard-hitting forwards Jason Leonard and Lawrence Dallaglio. I hesitate to use the expression 'hard-drinking' because they are certainly not that, but it is also true that the trio are among those who do not feel the need to pay total respect to the austere new severities around in the sport by refusing all alcohol.

We can certainly raise a glass to Guscott as a player. He is easily the greatest English back I have seen, stands alongside Gerald Davies and Campese – possibly even a little ahead of them both – for sheer, electric entertainment value. When the ball was two passes away from him, the whole match seemed to hit the supercharger. When he got it, it was rare for what happened next to be mundane. He was not only a glorious runner and brilliant passer. The key has been that he could transfer those talents to the highest level. Many backs have been good to watch, able to carve out breaks. Guscott was a match-winner, a series-winner, at British Lions level; in other words, at the roof of rugby.

Significant, too, was his contribution to the 1993 British Lions tour. He did not pull off any individual match-winning tricks, but he did achieve something which, as he told me at the time, was even more important. He proved that he was a defender, a hard man in the battle. He proved he could adapt in style. If my celestial team would pair up Guscott in the centre with the brilliant Frank Bunce of New Zealand, with each man at his peak, then I am equipped to win against any centre combination that the wide world of rugby has ever thrown up.

I'd seen Guscott as a fringe Bath player on a few occasions but never studied him for any length of time until I reported on a match between Pontypool and Bath at Pontypool Park on the very first Saturday of 1988-89 season, his first as a first-choice member of the first team. It was in those days when seasons began on 1 September, not at times when we were supposed to be still on the beaches having our summer holidays. It was also in those days when forward play made space for backs, not, as in modern rugby, when backs and forwards conspire together to clog the field up and shut down space for everybody. If there is a sadness about Guscott's latter career, it is definitely that rugby has changed so that genius is submerged in a general bish-bash mediocrity of style in which all-purpose players charge through endless phases. It isn't that he ever minded getting his hands dirty, but nowadays rugby requires its virtuoso concert pianists to shift the ruddy piano as well.

Back to Pontypool. The Gwent rottweilers had lost only four games in the whole of the previous season. Yet they were devastated, taken to pieces by a Bath back division in which Stuart Barnes and Simon Halliday were the catalysts, but in which Guscott ran gloriously, carving through outside with a pace, a wit and a style that took the breath away. It is not to blow my own trumpet – I am the man who predicted that New Zealand would beat France in the 1999 World Cup semi-final by more than 40 points, so I'm not putting myself forward as a rugby equivalent of *Old Moore's Almanack* – but in a report of that match, I did write: 'It seems as if it is the end of the Pontypool era. But it could well be the start of the Guscott era.' It was. By the end of that season he was an England international and a British Lion.

To catch Bath in that season was a joy. Guscott confessed afterwards that, in a sense, rugby was never so enjoyable, never gave him such freedom again. Barnes and Halliday were consummate. Halliday was able to take out both centres and get away his pass with such a facility that it was Guscott and Audley Lumsden, the full back, who scored dozens of tries between them. The breaks were usually so clean and overwhelming that the Bath wings were needed only for a kind of ceremonial shepherding as Guscott ran the ball in. Jack Rowell, the coach, was wise enough to give this back line of sublime class its head. Guscott was sheer brilliance. He lifted the whole game, he gave England rugby, essentially a hard-working and yet uninspired arena, a gem to treasure. The popularity of the man has never wavered since he first began to cut teams apart, beginning with poor old Ponty all those years ago.

The first season was nothing less than a smoothly accelerating path to glory. He was chosen for his first England cap against Romania in Bucharest, went gliding all around that giant stadium for three tries in England's thumping victory. At the time, I considered that it had been me who discovered him at Pontypool, so it was with a proprietorial pride that I saw him run in his hat-trick. A few weeks later, with injury striking the original Lions selection for their tour of Australia, he was chosen, became a Lion. It was obvious that Ian McGeechan, the coach, was suspicious of him in the early matches, and Guscott had not even a sniff of the Test team as the Lions subsided to defeat in Sydney in the 1st Test. But by the time of the 2nd Test, the vital, do-or-die match for the whole tour, McGeechan was beginning to believe. It was an admiration (a mutual admiration, too) that was to last and grow stronger through the three Lions tours the pair made together, and beyond.

The Lions took a precarious lead near the end of the 2nd Test in Brisbane, when came the killer blow. I can still feel the hair-raising tremor of excitement when we realised that Guscott, given the ball running left, was going to chip between the two Aussie centres. He chipped, chased, dived, scored. The Lions won. At the time, he was still a bricklayer. He never laid another brick.

Small wonder that there was a reaction. He never had time to draw breath in that whole brilliant inaugural year, from Pontypool to Twickenham to Bucharest to Brisbane. Nothing in his life would ever be the same again. At the start of the next season, he felt depressed, he keenly felt the lack of the usual thrill he felt when he set off for Bath games. It is another tribute to his strength of character that he was able to assess his own feelings so accurately and press on till the reaction faded and the energy and anticipation returned – even if the old joys were gone for good in a game which was by now setting traps for him. They never, however, tied him down completely.

His England career was not always so dramatic because England in his time have usually been a conservative team, but from all his England caps and from the fistful of Triple Crowns and Grand Slams, my favourite memory is of the England-Scotland match at Twickenham in 1993. Stuart Barnes, with whom he always felt most comfortable, was at fly half on a rare appearance in the middle of the Rob Andrew era. Barnes shot off on the break after seizing a high pass. It was a devastating burst, out of the blue. But Guscott had played with Barnes for so long, knew too much about Barnes to be surprised. Guscott, as he did so many times on so many grounds, was able to reach Barnes and be accelerating to top pace just as Barnes' momentum died.

I have written this more than once before, but when Barnes slipped him the ball I swear that Guscott was moving faster than anyone has ever moved on the rugby field. One instant, Scott Hastings was shaping to tackle him, next instant, he was five metres in his wake. Guscott held the ball beautifully, ran the perfect line, slipped Rory

Underwood over in the corner. Guscott seemed to get his breath back a long time before most of the onlookers. Wondrous. Nothing less.

There were down periods when injury afflicted him, the odd period out of favour, notably when Rowell jettisoned him in favour of Will Carling in a period when Phil de Glanville was England's other centre and captain. It was the one time I parted company with the estimable Rowell. The truth is that Carling was nothing like as brilliant a centre; the truth is also that, even though they played together for England so many times, the pair never even began to exist as a true, complementary partnership. The great Halliday formed a true, almost mystical partnership with Guscott, where things could be executed almost with an extra-sensory perception. It is a tragedy that the Barnes/Halliday/Guscott triumvirate was not given more rope by dull England managements.

The Lions, of course, treasured Guscott. He was still first-choice Test centre with the British Lions in South Africa in 1997, and played well throughout, notably in defence, as the Springboks battered the Lions almost to a pulp in the 2nd Test in Durban, with the first already, and sensationally, in the Lions' bag. Towards the end in Durban, though, the Lions somehow found the courage to battle back, and came to within one kick of the Springboks, to within one kick of winning the series.

Sometimes, Guscott causes a kind of rueful irritation. You love the bloke, but here he is again, making another effortless break, or scoring a brilliant hat-trick, or signing another big contract, or getting away with some heinous dressing-room offence because of his aura, or moving into another nice home which his Dad will do up for him and his wife refurbish, or being presented with yet another lovely daughter. Lucky bleeder. It was in this spirit that Wardle and Blackett, his mates, were watching the agonising closing stages of the Durban Test on the television back in Bath. 'I bet that bugger drops a goal now,' Wardle said as the match reached its height. Over it went, of course; the high drop, the series winner, the most famous kick by any British Isles player on any rugby field. Had to do it at the very end, after the agony and the pounding, of course. Less dramatic effect if you do it early.

Perhaps too much of this is in the past tense for a man still on active service, with a testimonial season to run through. It is not meant to read as an epitaph. I suppose the final challenge, however, is for Guscott to adjust to a life where the adrenalin from heroic sporting deeds is behind him, to find some role in rugby that is not merely as a conventional coach. However, since at heart there has always been an ordinary bloke underneath, since the real Guscott is the Bath family man, then to revert may not be so difficult as he himself, if he is honest, often fears. The process of adjustment has already begun, with appearances in the media as an expert summariser for the BBC.

He drew so much from rugby – it helped him overcome his youthful waywardness, found him a pastime and a career and allowed him to express superb talents. But I tend to think that rugby is in Guscott's debt, not the other way around. He has played in an era where rugby could be dull. But he has galvanised that era, done wonders for the sport's image, its marketability, its appeal to youngsters. He has reminded everyone that there is artistry among the thump of confrontation.

Perhaps the most fascinating stories he told when reminiscing on his career were those concerning not periods of his career or matches or seasons but micro-seconds. He had uncanny recall of those fractions of time which elapsed as he had the ball and decided his next move. When he was put away in space with Rory Underwood outside him in the 2nd Test in 1993, he ran on with John Kirwan, the All Black wing, coming across in defence. Guscott could recall the whole thing in a kind of frozen motion – how he knew he had to hold on to the ball, show it to Kirwan, veer towards him to keep him interested so that Kirwan could not merely shadow Guscott then shift on to Underwood outside to make the tackle. 'I had to commit him, and to do that I had to make him look at me. As soon as he looked, I passed to Rory and Rory was clear.' It was astonishing to watch the video of that move again and realise how short the time frame was.

Similarly, he expounded once on two of his favourite tries, in an era when he was new and unknown on the circuit. He scored two dazzling individual efforts against Swansea at St Helen's and remarkably he could remember everything about the runs, the people veering towards him in his peripheral vision, the changes of line he had to make. Again, it was a recall of frozen moments and a quiet pride in matters which gave him more satisfaction, frankly, than the more arcane of rugby duties. 'It was running free,' he said of those early days and those Swansea scores.

But there is no doubt whatsoever as to my favourite Guscott story, the best that wound itself on to that whirring interview tape. By the time he went on the 1989 Lions tour, still as a tyro in international terms, he and Henry were getting on far better. In fact, they were friends again as a prelude to establishing the normal father-and-son relationship. Henry was watching the 2nd Test match on television in the pre-dawn of a Bath summer morning, sharing the anxiety of the occasion as the Lions battled to save the series. Then Guscott played his masterstroke, the chip and chase and the final dive to level the series and set up the triumphs a week later.

Henry was bursting with adrenalin when the match ended, but had no outlet. He was almost helpless, with no pub or club bar to unwind in and share the glory of the moment. So he went to find his sledgehammer, strode out of his house and down the hill to where Jeremy lived. In the house was a wall that Jeremy and Jayne had decided was not needed in their plans to redevelop the house. Henry attacked the wall with his sledgehammer, knocked it into small pieces, swept up the mess. Then he strode back up the hill to his own house.

It was a marvellous image. It reflected the celebrations of a brilliant British rugby victory in an era in which Jeremy Guscott was to be personally responsible for injecting sorely needed swagger and self-belief. It reflected the final disappearance of the barriers which had grown up between father and son, also reflected Henry's pride; and the disappearance of the final barriers separating Jeremy Guscott from true sporting greatness.

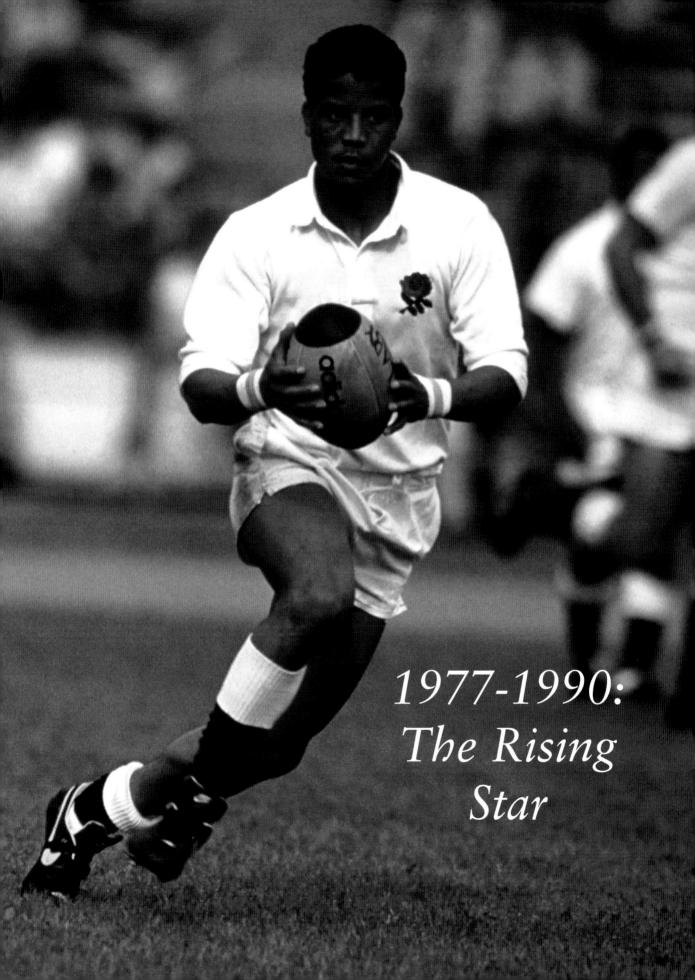

1977-1990:
The Rising
Star

ABOVE My long association with Bath could be said to have begun in the early 1970s, when I began playing rugby for the minis. But the Bath years are not an unbroken line. The club did not run youth teams between 11 and 16, so for those formative years we all moved up to Walcot Old Boys. A sort of 'Bath in exile', Walcot used to rent Lambridge, Bath's second ground. The Walcot days were great days. Every year we seemed to have a tiny team, far smaller than the opposition. We seemed to be various bits of riff-raff thrown together to play against well-organised rugby teams. But we played with tremendous heart, we loved the concept of playing for each other. I sometimes managed a jinking kind of try from my normal position as fly half, and when we won, it was a fantastic feeling. We enjoyed the team spirit in adversity, a factor which saw both Walcot and Bath teams through in my later career. Tony Wardle, who with Peter Blackett was to be joint best man at my wedding, was in the team. We used to go up to the ground together to play, on

Sundays, and revelled in it. When the time came to return to Bath, when I was invited to train with them at the age of 16, it was a wrench to leave. The club have always kept in touch, sending me messages of congratulations at various points in my subsequent career, and I owe them a debt of gratitude.

Jeremy Guscott, third from right in the back row, photographed with his Walcot Old Boys Colts team-mates in 1977, in the grounds of Ralph Allen Comprehensive School, which Guscott attended for a time. Standing next to Guscott, second from the right in the back row, is Tony 'Chalkie' Wardle, Jeremy's joint best man and captain of Walcot Old Boys for the 2000-2001 season. Next to Wardle is Keith 'Kipper' Jones, who, according to a Walcot source, 'taught young Jerry to kick the ball properly'. At the left-hand end of the back row, alongside coach Roy Beddoe, is Gary Frankcom, who also went on to Bath, while kneeling at the left-hand end of the front row is Simon Chambers, captain of Walcot Old Boys 2nd XV in 2000-2001.

ABOVE I was playing some games at fly half for Bath 2nd XV by the mid-1980s. With John Horton expected to retire at the end of the 1984-85 season, it seemed that I was in a queue of three for the 1st XV fly half position, along with Charles Gabbitas and Alun Watkins. *In January 1985, the same month that this photo of Bath United, the Bath 2nd XV, was taken, the 19-year-old Guscott made his 1st XV debut at Waterloo. The omens were good: he played not at fly half but in the centre.*
RIGHT On a tour to Boston in 1985, Bath played in an international tournament. At the end of the final, we were losing but we had a chance to take the title with a long penalty. Roger Spurrell, the captain, whose commitment bordered on the dangerous, gave me the Spurrell look. 'You are going to take it and you are going to get it,' he said. If I had missed it, I wouldn't be here today. I kicked it and Bath won.
The Bath party gathers in May 1985 prior to the tour to Boston, Massachusetts.

ABOVE The 1984-85 JPS Cup final was fairly nerve-racking. I was only 19, and to go on and play at Twickenham was pretty much a dream. I had the mickey taken out of me for something I said after the game. My friends and I used to refer to each other as 'bloods', as they did in comedy films – 'Hey, blood, how you going?' and that kind of stuff. Being young and naive, when Nigel Starmer-Smith interviewed me in the tunnel after the game, I sent a message via the interview to a couple of friends, Pete Blackett and Chalkie Wardle. I can't remember what question Nigel asked me, but I just said, 'Yeah, the blood done it.' It was really corny, but at the time I was pumped up – I'd got on and played in a John Player Special Cup final and won and was part of the team.

Guscott in action against London Welsh in the 1984-85 JPS Cup final, his first, which Bath won 24-15. He came on as replacement for Barry Trevaskis and played the second half in the unfamiliar position of wing.

RIGHT Centre was my position by 1985-86, but I was still in a queue – behind John Palmer and Simon Halliday. These two Bath legends were the first-choice centres at the club in the mid-1980s, so I made only occasional first-team appearances during this period. *The Bath 1st XV prepare to charge down a kick late in the 1986-87 season. The visible players are, from left to right, Tony Swift (beyond the posts), Simon Halliday (partially hidden behind Guscott), Guscott himself, Chris Martin, Andy Robinson, Gareth Chilcott, Chris Lilley, Dave Egerton, John Morrison and Barry Trevaskis.*

BELOW RIGHT I don't remember anything about the 1986-87 JPS Cup final, only that Wasps at that time had a lot of internationals, so I would have been pretty nervous. They had people like Huw Davies, Kevin Simms [No. 13], who was an England centre at the time, and Rob Andrew at No. 10.
Guscott accepts a pass during the 1986-87 final, in which Bath defeated Wasps 19-12. He had not played in the 1985-86 cup final win, also over Wasps, and this time was a replacement for Tony Swift after 48 minutes.

BELOW Here I'm providing back-up for full back Chris Martin, as Nick Maslen (right) and John Morrison arrive in support. John had spent the previous summer in Wollongong, New South Wales, with a club called the Waratahs. The summer of 1987 was to see me installed as an overseas player with the same club.
Bath v Bristol, April 1987.

PREVIOUS PAGE In 1987-88, I finally became a regular in the Bath 1st XV. However, it wasn't until the season after that that I became a first-choice centre, alongside Simon Halliday, when John Palmer's commitments as a schoolmaster led to him scaling down his appearances. *Scenes from the 1988-89 season, in which Bath completed their first double by winning the Pilkington Cup (formerly the John Player Special Cup) and the Courage League title. Playing outside Stuart Barnes and Simon Halliday, Guscott ran in 28 first-class tries.*

RIGHT 'Coochie' [Gareth Chilcott] said the same thing, every match, every season, when talking about our next opponents. 'They are big, strong and robust.' We met so many teams that were big, strong and robust that it is a wonder we ever won a match. *Guscott, Chilcott and Nigel Redman celebrate Bath's 6-3 away victory over Gloucester in the 1988-89 Pilkington Cup semi-finals.*

BELOW The best thing about playing in the cup final was that you got a suit made up, which didn't often happen as an amateur rugby player. Also, you went up the night before and stayed in a really nice hotel. One of the thank-yous after having a hard season and for getting to the cup final was that everybody got to raise the trophy and hear the cheers from the supporters. That was a great moment. *Jeremy Guscott with the Pilkington Cup after Bath beat Leicester 10-6 in the 1988-89 final, Stuart Barnes scoring all his side's points, including the only try of the game. This was Guscott's first start in a Twickenham cup final.*

LEFT AND BELOW The best thing about my England debut was that I was playing alongside Simon Halliday [left, with Guscott and Rory Underwood]. Most people at the time thought that that should have been the England partnership anyway. Also playing was Gareth Chilcott, so I had club colleagues around me. All of my family came out, as well as Jayne, who was my fiancée at the time. Everybody cut the sleeves off their shirts, but because that was my first England game, I couldn't destroy my England shirt, so in the photograph I've got my sleeves rolled up. It was just a great occasion. All I remember about it is that a lot of the times I got the ball, there was a gap to run through, so I just ran, and it opened up. I'd like to think that anybody else who was in that position would have been able to do it as well. It's just that it happened for me, which was great. Romania was a strange place to go. They were handing out bottles of Coke in the hotel that were covered in dust, as though they'd been there for centuries. From 5 o'clock or half past five, the streets were deserted, just the odd car zooming through junctions. Apart from that there was nothing going on whatsoever. It was a weird experience but a good one.

Jeremy Guscott played his first match for England against Romania in Bucharest on 13 May 1989. He scored three tries in England's 58-3 victory.

passenger request: _Spoil me_

Delta BusinessElite®:

5 courses of tasty things to eat
a fine wine (or two)
all the films you've been meaning to see, TV and your kind of music
a serve yourself snack table
ice-cream sundaes so huge they're sinful

▲**Delta**

fly 5-Star

See your travel agent or call 0800 414 767

delta-air.com

*Passengers with hand luggage only

ABOVE Being chosen for the 1989 Lions was all part of a weird weekend. Within about four days, Bath won the cup against Leicester, I was selected to replace Will Carling for England and then selected for the Lions, which was just awesome.
Guscott fells Wallaby wing Ian Williams during the 1989 Australia v British Lions Test series.

RIGHT I was sub for the game against NSW. I'd been out with a few of the 'dirt-trackers'. I'd promised myself that I'd only drink a couple of cans of Tooheys and the rest of the night I'd drink Coke. Well, by about midnight that had all gone out the window. I think I walked in at about four in the morning. There was a knock on the door at about half past eight from Ian McGeechan, saying that Brendan Mullin had pulled out and I was playing. I didn't really give him time to linger because I think he would have smelled my breath, so I quickly said 'Oh! Great! Fantastic!' and slammed the door and thought 'What am I going to do?' Kevin Murphy was the Lions physio on that tour, and he saw me walk in and just couldn't believe the state I was in and how I looked. He managed to revitalise me and got me into shape, and I went out and played pretty well.
Jeremy Guscott takes off against New South Wales at the North Sydney Oval on 24 June 1989. The Lions triumphed 23-21.

ABOVE AND LEFT It didn't happen in slow motion at the time, but I've always been a fairly instinctive player. I got the ball and I didn't feel there was anything else on other than to dribble it through. Luckily, I think it was a prop there and I managed to slip by him. Then I think it was a race between me and Michael Lynagh, who was back-tracking. The ball just sat up so nicely for me and I scored the try. We were winning the game, but that just sealed it. We were thinking, 'Right, we can go on to the next game and really have a go'. It just set us up, really – a great feeling. It's an achievement to get selected for the Lions squad. It's even better to play in a Test match. And then to score a try... The next thing after that is to drop a goal that wins a series, I suppose.

Guscott beats Michael Lynagh to touch down late in the 2nd Test between the Lions and Australia at Ballymore, Brisbane, on 8 July 1989, then celebrates his masterstroke with scrum half Robert Jones. The Lions won the match 19-12. Watching his son's try live at home in Bath in the early hours was Henry Guscott. He could not contain his excitement at what he had just seen, so he went down to his son's new house and demolished an unwanted kitchen wall with a sledgehammer!

ABOVE RIGHT *Jeremy lines up with skipper Finlay Calder (centre) and David Sole during the 3rd Test.*

RIGHT *The Lions celebrate after beating Australia 19-18 at the Sydney Football Stadium to win the 3rd Test and the series. In so doing, they became the first successful Lions since Willie-John McBride's side defeated South Africa in 1974.*

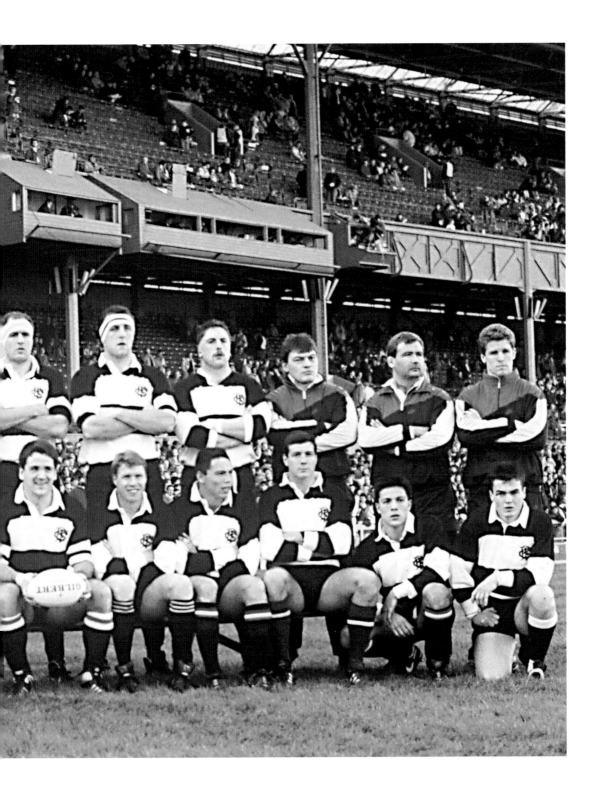

PREVIOUS PAGES The Barbarians match against a New Zealand XV in 1989 was another good occasion because the Lions had come back from a successful tour and McGeechan felt that by the last Test we were just hitting form and that it would have been nice to have gone across to New Zealand and had a crack at those boys. So the Barbarians were pretty much a Lions team, plus Nick Farr-Jones but without Finlay Calder. It was nice to play in that old Twickenham ground because everything was so close to you. You really felt your support was there.

The New Zealand XV beat the Barbarians 21-10 on 25 November 1989. Craig Innes, Zinzan Brooke and Richard Loe crossed the line for the men in black, and Grant Fox kicked three conversions and a penalty. Philip Matthews scored a try in reply for the Baa Baas, and Gavin Hastings slotted two penalties. Back row (left to right): Colin Stephens, Fergus Aherne, Gary Jones, Jeremy Guscott, Gary Rees, Philip Matthews, Paul Ackford, Wade Dooley, Phil Davies. Steve Smith, Des Fitzgerald, Brendan Mullin Front row: Gavin Hastings, David Young, Brian Moore, David Sole, Nick Farr-Jones, Rory Underwood, Scott Hastings, Tony Underwood (uncapped at the time), Tony Clement.

LEFT We won the 1989 game against Fiji quite easily. However, we were playing 'tortoise rugby', where you pass and then you duck, because we knew they were coming in and they would hit us bloody hard. It was a comfortable game, we played some half-decent rugby, but it was an experience. You get hit by those guys, you're never going to get hit harder again in your life! *Three weeks before the Barbarians v New Zealand XV game, England had played the Fijian tourists at headquarters and beaten them 58-23, with Guscott being one of five England players to score a single try while Rory Underwood was racking up five! Here Guscott tries to capitalise on Will Carling's tackle as Fijian full back Naituilagilagi moves in. Two Fijians were sent off during this match.*

light fantastic

Giro 500   £599.99

worth more than a try

DAWES
DISCOVER YOUR WORLD

RIGHT I think many people thought I would be up and away from British Gas very rapidly. However, I remained with them for more than five years. It took me time to be accepted, but I think my colleagues recognised that I was trying to be as successful with my business life as I had been in sport.

Jeremy Guscott at work in the offices of British Gas South Western, whose PR department he joined in January 1990. He eventually moved into marketing during a long stay with the company, who were happy to grant him time off to pursue his rugby activities.

BELOW It was a great game, my first Five Nations match at Twickenham, and of course it was great to score a try. It was just a fantastic game of rugby, where I don't think we were ever pushed that hard. We cruised to a win that should have been more. It was about timing and running into space. All I did was just get the ball and accelerate and everything opened up. It was just nice to score a try on my Five Nations debut at Twickenham.

Jeremy Guscott runs in his try as England beat Ireland 23-0 in the 1989-90 Five Nations Championship.

ABOVE I don't actually know what's going on in this picture. No one of about 13 stone, as I was then, who was in their right mind would have taken on the sheep farmer from Kelso, Mr Jeffrey. That game was strange. I didn't really understand at the time what was at stake. You realised at the end by looking at some of the more experienced players how big a loss it was. The media, as ever, made us huge favourites, forgetting that Scotland had put in some very good performances along the way. There were also a number of Lions players in each squad. For us, it didn't happen. A bit disappointing but not the end of the world.

Action as Scotland beat England 13-7 at Murrayfield to win the 1990 Grand Slam decider. Guscott scored England's try. To be fair to the parties here, a previous frame suggests that all are involved not in argy-bargy but in a desperate struggle for a loose ball.

LEFT Everyone had a licence to do what he wanted to in this game. I scored one try. I sidestepped and danced my way through maybe about five or six people. On the way back I got to the halfway line and bowed to Prince Edward, as if to say 'I hope you enjoyed that'. It was a game of enjoyment to raise money, which we were all pleased to be part of.

A Four Home Unions XV beat a Rest of Europe XV 43-18 at Twickenham on 22 April 1990. The game was played in aid of Rugby for Romania.

RIGHT AND BELOW The 1989-90 Pilkington final was a great cup final because it was a local derby at Twickenham. There was a full house and everybody expected it to be pretty close but we just ran away with it. It was just a great day. It was also really hot. I made a break and then passed on to Tony Swift, but I passed too early, which meant the cover could get to him – so then he passed it back to me. Normally, you passed to Swifty and it was try, so I'd kind of switched off a little bit. And then I realised I'd messed up, so I actually had to carry on running in support, and then got the pass inside for a score.

Bath won the 1989-90 Pilkington Cup final 48-6, Guscott being one of seven Bath players to get his name on the scoresheet. His centre partner Simon Halliday, with Guscott below, was a winner again at Twickenham the following year with Harlequins.

FOLLOWING PAGES *Guscott brings down Gloucester full back Tim Smith during the 1989-90 final. The other Bath player in view is Tony Swift, who scored two tries in the game, one an individual effort that saw him sprint virtually the length of the field. The story goes that the reason Swift made it to the line was that he was terrified of being caught by his opposite number, who had a reputation as a fearsome tackler.*

1991-1995:
The Grand
Slam Years

Hong Kong is a special place to go. It's just a unique atmosphere. It's just carnival, festival, high spirits. It's just huge appreciation. Different cultures coming together and playing each other. Everybody used to parade at the opening. I remember in 1990 the Scottish guys walked round and they were in kilts. They bent over and each had a letter on his bum that spelt out 'GRAND SLAM'.

LEFT *The Barbarians squad that contested the 1990 Hong Kong Sevens competition. From front to rear: Brian Moore, Richard Moon, Rob Andrew, Will Carling, Barry Evans, Peter Winterbottom, Jeremy Guscott, Chris Sheasby.*

RIGHT *In action against Germany during the 1991 tournament. Neil Back is in the background. That year, the Baa Baas beat Australia in the quarter-finals but lost 22-14 to eventual winners Fiji in the semis.*

BELOW *The 1991 Baa Baas squad, complete with lambs. Clockwise from left: Will Carling, Ian Hunter, Micky Skinner, Andrew Harriman, Rupert Moon, Chris Sheasby, Neil Back, Jeremy Guscott, Tony Underwood.*

BELOW LEFT *Closer to home this time. Playing for Bath against Blackheath II in the 1990 Middlesex Sevens.*

The future is in your hands.

Sound advice for your future from
leading business advisors, KPMG.

Contact Richard Boot on 0121 232 3000.

www.kpmg.co.uk

It's time for clarity.

ABOVE The most memorable thing about this match was Federico Mendez being sent off for smacking Paul Ackford. Paul had the mickey taken out of him so much by the rest of the forwards. Mendez was only 18.
Jeremy Guscott tackles Diego Cuesta Silva of Argentina during England's 51-0 victory at Twickenham in November 1990. England full back Simon Hodgkinson, covering, set a new England points-scoring record (23) in this game.

RIGHT That's the only time I used to get dirty, by scoring a try like this.
A prostrate Guscott after scoring one of his two tries in the Argentina game.

FOLLOWING PAGES *On the club scene, Bath won the 1990-91 Courage League, their second title, finishing three points ahead of Wasps. Here Bath celebrate lifting the championship after their 49-6 demolition of Saracens away from home. Back row (left to right): Jon Webb, Jim Fallon, Andy Robinson, Jeremy Guscott (who scored twice in the match), Steve Ojomoh, Nigel Redman (partially obscured), Victor Ubogu, Stuart Barnes (captain), Martin Haag, Jon Hall, Graham Dawe. Front row: Tony Swift, Gareth Chilcott, Phil de Glanville, Richard Hill.*

1991

We knew in 1991 that we were much stronger up front than most teams, so we just pummelled them, basically. We kept it tight, went down the lines, got in positions to score, and scored.

LEFT *The England team photographed for the England v France 1991 Five Nations Grand Slam decider at Twickenham. Back row (left to right): Simon Halliday (replacement), Jon Webb (replacement), Rory Underwood, Peter Winterbottom, Mike Teague, Paul Ackford, Wade Dooley, Dean Richards, Jeff Probyn, Jason Leonard, Mick Skinner (replacement), Dewi Morris (replacement). Front row: Paul Rendall (replacement), Nigel Heslop, Brian Moore, Richard Hill, Will Carling (captain), Rob Andrew, Jeremy Guscott, Simon Hodgkinson, John Olver (replacement).*

BELOW LEFT *After their 25-6 defeat of Wales in Cardiff in the opening round, England had the next Five Nations weekend off before facing Scotland at Twickenham. Here Jeremy Guscott takes on the Scots during the match, which England won 21-12. A 16-7 victory in Dublin a fortnight later brought Carling's team to the brink again.*

RIGHT *No mistake this time. Guscott and Will Carling congratulate Rory Underwood on his try in the 21-19 win over France, which brought England their first Grand Slam since 1980.*

BELOW It was good, it was satisfying but not total. It was good to do it in '91 because of what happened in '90, because most of us had experienced defeat and losing the Grand Slam. It was essential that we came back and won it, and we did.
A happy, and possibly relieved, England team drink to their Grand Slam triumph.

ABOVE I love Australia as a country. Brisbane at that time was my favourite place. Coming from Bath, which is quite small, I thought Sydney was too big, but Brisbane was quiet and not so fast-moving. And it was a return to Ballymore, where I'd scored the try in '89. *Jeremy Guscott takes on the Queensland defence at Ballymore during England's tour of Australia and Fiji in July 1991. Guscott scored one of England's three tries, but the home side eventually triumphed 20-14.*

LEFT Again, the Fiji game was pretty scary because you were playing against these guys who swing in at shoulder level at the lowest, so it was a question of looking after yourself. It was played in Suva, with a huge crowd. It was quite intimidating, very, very hot, very, very humid. Mike Teague played and he'd had a terrible tummy bug. At half-time, he was so weak he declared, 'I can't go on'. However, because of the banter between the boys, instead of being sympathetic, everybody got stuck into him for being such a wimp. This was 'Iron Mike' Teague saying things like that! *Guscott breaks out in the Test against Fiji on 20 July 1991, which England won 28-12.*

RIGHT Having a bit of a laugh on the tour with the journos who came along to watch the training sessions. Every now and again, the guys would ask to have a look through the lens while the forwards were training. *Having moved from Australia to Fiji for the Test match and a game against Fiji B, England returned to Australia for further matches.*

BELOW We got thrashed 40-15 by a good Australian side, although I did score a try. I was going down the touch line and all I saw was Willie Ofahengaue coming for me, so I pretended to really sprint hard, then I stopped and let him just carry on by. I think if he'd connected with me he'd have knocked me into the '95 World Cup, let alone the '91 competition. *Guscott is pursued by Tim Horan and Jason Little during the Test at the Sydney Football Stadium on 27 July.*

Daily Mail

The Daily Mail is delighted to support Jeremy Guscott and wishes him every success in the future

LEFT *A publicity picture with Ieuan Evans on behalf of Lotto, the official boot for the 1991 Rugby World Cup.*

BELOW There was a lot of hype about this match. It was the first game of the 1991 World Cup and we just froze a little bit. I don't think we believed we could actually win – and we didn't. Things just didn't happen. We were a bit stifled. Obviously you give the opposition respect, but we gave them too much respect, believing that they were a far better side than us, when in reality we were a lot closer than we thought.

Guscott sets up the ball for Dean Richards against New Zealand in England's opening match of the 1991 Rugby World Cup. Played on 3 October at Twickenham, the match resulted in an 18-12 victory for the All Blacks, their flanker Michael Jones scoring the game's only try.

ABOVE Italy were not renowned for their open, attractive rugby and gave away a load of penalties. We didn't play fantastically ourselves, because we were restricted. I scored a couple of tries in that game. In one of them, the ball was kicked to one of our players, who passed to me, and I just ran straight, then veered off left towards the South Stand. Then it was just a straight sprint for the corner, and I managed to get there first.

Guscott looks around for support as he is brought to a halt during England's 36-6 victory over Italy at Twickenham in their second pool match of the 1991 World Cup. England went on to beat the USA 37-9 in their final pool match (in which Simon Halliday occupied Guscott's centre berth) to finish second in the group behind New Zealand.

LEFT We never really looked back after the New Zealand match. We just got better and better until the final.

Guscott celebrates England's 19-10 quarter-final win over France at Parc des Princes. England then went to Murrayfield for their semi-final, where they defeated Scotland 9-6.

Before the final, I don't know for what reason, we started subconsciously taking notice of the media. They were saying we weren't going to get many chances against this side and England might have to change, or should change, the way they'd been playing. We trained thinking that we weren't going to get a lot of ball, so it was to be thrown out wide and we were to play a little bit looser than we had been. I've not looked at the stats, but I'm pretty sure Wade Dooley and Paul Ackford took more than their fair share of ball. Probably if we had played the way we had through that championship it would have been a lot closer. It's impossible to say we would have won. I'm at the end of my career now, and I sometimes think 'You came that close to winning a World Cup'. When there's an international football championship on, there's footage of the guys in 1966 and what it meant. Winning would have been huge, there's no doubt about it, but it wasn't to be.

LEFT AND BELOW *Action from the 1991 Rugby World Cup final at Twickenham, which Australia won 12-6.*

SARACENS

With best wishes to Jeremy
and with many thanks for
the many years of talent and pleasure
he's given to the game
from all at the Saracens

RIGHT When we won the league in 1991-92, we finished level on points with Orrell but took the title on points difference. We had been docked a point for failing to register a player, and that angered the team enough to ensure our trophy.

Jeremy Guscott in action in Feburary 1992 against Northampton, who finished third, just one point adrift of Bath and Orrell. Bath won this encounter 13-9.

BELOW It was a very, very close game. And for Barnesie to go for the drop was pretty spectacular. It wasn't a bad old whack, actually. It was the last play of the match, and it was a case of 'Well, what are we going to do?' 'Well, you've got to go for the drop, Barnesie.' 'Oh, I might be a little bit too far out.' 'Nah, I think you've got the bottle to do it.' Anyway, he got the ball, and 'bang', it went through. It was the sweetest feeling. And to beat Quins as well, because they play just across the road at The Stoop. It's about the only game I've ever seen when Peter Winterbottom was knocked backwards – by Victor Ubogu. Those are the two main reasons I remember it – Barnesie's dropped goal and the fact that Victor ran into Peter Winterbottom who normally nails people and just bumped him onto his backside. He won't be happy with me saying that!

Guscott congratulates Stuart Barnes on the dropped goal that separated Bath and Harlequins after they had stood at 12-12 with just seconds of extra time left on the clock. Gareth Chilcott is on his way to join the celebrations. Bath had now added the Pilkington Cup to the Courage League to complete their second double.

LEFT Webby was a good guy to play with. He was also a proper working professional outside of rugby, which was fairly unusual, because most of us had jobs that were very flexible, whereas Webby, being a doctor, couldn't miss out on too much. He was a guy I used to like to see drunk, because it was so unusual because of the work that he did. But when he'd had a few gin and tonics he was quite funny.
Guscott and Jon Webb, who was to have a superb Five Nations, training with England in January 1992.

BELOW We were favourites again that year and I don't think many sides came to Twickenham with a lot of confidence that they were going to have it easy.
Guscott, who scored in the game, is held in check this time in England's 38-9 win over Ireland at Twickenham.

ABOVE RIGHT There was one moment when Mick Skinner tackled their hooker and just knocked him for six. Skins is remembered for the tackle he made in Paris in the 1991 World Cup, but I remember this one more.
Guscott, with Skinner in support, hands on during England's 31-13 victory in Paris, in which two Frenchmen were sent off.

BELOW RIGHT *Jeremy Guscott takes on Scott Gibbs and Ieuan Evans as England subdue Wales 24-0 at Twickenham to record their first back-to-back Grand Slams since 1923 and 1924.*

LEFT It's always nice to win the league after a long, hard season. There's a good bunch of boys here, including Brian Ashton, then coach, Jon Callard, who's now the coach, Ben Clarke, on his first visit to Bath, Gareth Chilcott still playing, Jon Hall, and Andy Robinson holding the trophy.
Bath celebrate winning the 1992-93 Courage League title, after beating Saracens away on the last weekend.

TOP AND ABOVE We all got on the champagne and as a result this is what happened. We knew that the bungee thing was out there and I said, 'Oh, I think I'll do that'. The changing room went silent and everybody's head turned towards me, and I thought, 'There's no way I can bottle out of this'.
Guscott bungees at Saracens. Stuart Barnes, who jumped backwards, kept him company.

ABOVE Lanzarote, to me, was always like Colditz, like some sort of prison for hard training. But it was a necessity, something we had to do. There were some opportunities to have a drink, but if you drank you suffered the next day.
Guscott pounds the track at the England training camp at Lanzarote, in preparation for the 1993 Five Nations.

RIGHT *Closed down by Neil Jenkins and Mike Rayer during England's 10-9 defeat by Wales in Cardiff.*

BELOW *Scoring one of England's three tries in the 26-12 victory over Scotland at Twickenham.*

FOLLOWING PAGES *Guscott gets the ball away, despite the attentions of Camberabero, Sella and friend in the 16-15 defeat of eventual champions, France, in Paris.*

I enjoyed the 1993 trip to New Zealand. Socially, it was a fantastic tour, but as for success it wasn't great. We started off really well and won the first four games. I was enjoying it, having a good time. I didn't really feel I was definitely going to get in the Test team, so I was trying to prove a point along the way. It was my first chance to play with Scott Gibbs, which I thoroughly enjoyed. I suppose the thing that was talked about at the beginning was whether Will Carling was going to be captain, then Gavin became it. That was the main talking point before we went. When we got there we worked particularly hard and got ourselves in good shape, then an appalling refereeing decision in the 1st Test allowed Grant Fox to kick a penalty and win the game. That tour could have been so different, but that's sport. Sometimes the decisions don't go your way.

ABOVE LEFT The clay pigeon shooting was a bit scary. I remember Richard Webster had a pump-action shotgun. He was swinging it down by his legs and he let a round off, which missed Peter Winterbottom's foot by maybe two or three inches. There are different ways of trying to get into the Test team, but that's bordering on the ridiculous.
Guscott shoots clays on a day off.

LEFT The game against Canterbury was a good match for me. I think it pretty much clinched my Test spot. After a simple move, Gibbs busted through and I supported him and then just had to sprint to the line. There are very few games I can actually remember a lot of. Along with the 1993 England v Scotland match – when Stuart Barnes made the break that helped me send in Rory Underwood for his try – this is one of them, because I had a lot of involvement.
About to score in the 28-10 win over Canterbury.

BELOW *The 1993 Lions photocall.*

RIGHT Pretty well everything is forgotten about the 1st Test other than the last-minute decision the referee made. He reckoned Dean Richards had tackled the bloke and rolled over on the wrong side.
Guscott bears down on New Zealand's John Timu in the 1st Test, which the All Blacks won 20-18.

BELOW We lost the game against Auckland. Scott Gibbs and I started at centre. Will Carling came on to replace Gavin Hastings at full back, and he didn't play particularly well. That was the beginning of the end for Will on that trip, really.
Guscott about to pass to Scott Gibbs, as Rob Andrew and Rory Underwood look on. Auckland beat the Lions 23-18.

FOLLOWING PAGES Every time you beat the All Blacks is a great feeling because it doesn't happen very often, so it was great to win and it was good to stick Rory Underwood in for a try. He was a bit gutted because I think he dived and winded himself. There was a good celebration afterwards in the changing room. Also, we had a nice crew of people following us around New Zealand, which was great, so a lot of the guys went outside – well, Dean Richards went outside – and sang with the crowd in appreciation of their support.
The Lions celebrate their 20-7 victory in the 2nd Test at Wellington. They could not repeat their success in the 3rd Test at Auckland, going down 30-13 to lose the series.

It was early November 1993, and I had only played a few matches for Bath. The injury I was carrying in my pelvic region had caused me problems for several months, and was now agony if I so much as turned over in bed, got in or out of a car or even walked along the street. It was a condition that was to keep me out of rugby until October 1994.

FAR LEFT, TOP *Playing for Bath against the touring South African Barbarians at the start of the 1993-94 season, in a match the visitors won 34-23.*

FAR LEFT, BOTTOM *Scoring Bath's second try in their 46-17 demolition of Gloucester at the Rec, another of the few appearances Guscott made in 1993-94.*

LEFT *The subject of a photographic profile in his home town of Bath in September 1993 before injury struck.*

BELOW *Receiving the 1994 Yardley English Blazer Award for the best-dressed sportsman. He took the vote ahead of boxer Chris Eubank, golfer Nick Faldo, and footballers Barry Venison and Ian Wright.*

Ferraris Group plc
congratulate Jeremy Guscott
on an outstanding rugby career
with Bath, England and the Lions
and wish him every success in the future.

LEFT AND BELOW This is one that the media people really enjoyed because they were all looking forward to going to their normal local places, that weren't too far to travel to. Then suddenly it was announced that I was coming back, so they all had to make the trip up to West Hartlepool, which they weren't all too happy about. But it was good to be back playing after such a long time off.

Jeremy Guscott makes his comeback from injury, playing for Bath against West Hartlepool on 18 October 1994. Bath were victors by 20 points to 18.

RIGHT It was nice to get back and play, and play well enough for the club that I was able to get selected again for England. Everything just carried on, where I suppose there was always a danger that it might not. I suppose it was ironic that my England debut was against Romania and my comeback game was against them as well.

Guscott makes his England comeback on 12 November 1994 at Twickenham, being paired with Will Carling in the centre for a world record 29th time in major internationals. England defeated Romania 54-3.

BELOW Everybody thought this final was going to be a bit tighter than it was, but we played some good rugby and basically deserved to win. It seemed that every time we played at Twickenham the sun was shining. It was a glorious day, and just a great outing again. Nothing much changed – every time we went to Twickenham, we won. And every cup final we've played in we've won.

Guscott's comeback season of 1994-95 was topped off with another Bath victory in the Pilkington Cup final at Twickenham. Here he is on the attack during the match – incidentally Tony Swift's last for the club – in which Bath beat Wasps 36-16.

LEFT I got a bit of stick in this game because near the end I'd been looking for a try and I hadn't scored. Anyway, I went for it and got caught a yard short, so all the questions were starting to come out – Guscott's injury has taken his pace away and all that kind of stuff. I tried to ignore it, but the more it goes on, the more it starts grating at you. But we won.

Guscott contests a high ball with Ireland's Niall Hogan (right) and Niall Woods in England's 20-8 victory in Dublin – the first leg of their 1995 Grand Slam.

BELOW *Guscott tries to outpace Wales captain, and fellow British Lion, Ieuan Evans at Cardiff. England won this encounter 23-9.*

ABOVE RIGHT I hadn't scored for a while, so to score against France at Twickenham was nice. I threw a dummy and just scraped through. It was a case of put the ball down and salute the South Stand. Another good moment.

Guscott evades Deylaud to touch down under the posts, with referee Ken McCartney ideally placed. The match result was an England victory by 31 points to 10.

RIGHT It was good to win the Grand Slam again, under Jack Rowell this time. At the time, you don't really realise what's going on, but it's nice to be able to look back and say, 'I was part of three Grand Slams for England'.

Guscott gets the champagne treatment after the 24-12 win over Scotland at Twickenham that brought England their third Grand Slam of the 1990s.

LEFT Phil de Glanville probably hitting me harder than he should, thinking he should be playing instead of me. There was always good banter between Phil and me. Come the World Cup, I didn't play my best rugby, and I suppose there was a call for Phil to be playing instead of me, but I was picked. That's just the way it went. *Guscott training with Bath colleague Phil de Glanville at Johannesburg during the 1995 Rugby World Cup.*

BELOW *Guscott challenges Matt Burke during the England v Australia RWC quarter-final at Cape Town.*

RIGHT That's probably the fastest Rob's run, after dropping that goal. If he'd run as fast as that on a number of occasions he might have scored a few more tries. When he struck it, I just went 'I can't believe it. That's gone'. He smacked it. It was so sweet. It's a shame that wasn't the final and we'd got our full revenge on Australia. But it's just a moment you can't really say too much about, because it's full of emotion. *Joy for Guscott and Rob Andrew as the fly half's injury-time dropped goal attempt sails home from 45 metres to make the score 25-22 and put England in the semi-finals.*

BELOW RIGHT We just got blown out of the water. Thankfully, I was nowhere near Lomu in that game. He was just on fire. I know Will made some comment afterwards calling him a freak, but I think he meant it in the way that the guy was 20 years old, 18 stone and ran as fast as Rory and Tony Underwood, and that'd just never been seen before. That match was summed up when Zinzan Brooke dropped a goal. When it went over we thought, 'Well, it's definitely not our day'. *Guscott makes a break as England go down 45-29 to New Zealand in the 1995 World Cup semis.*

The future is in your hands.

Sound advice for your future from leading business advisors, KPMG.

Contact Richard Boot on 0121 232 3000.

www.kpmg.co.uk

It's time for clarity.

ABOVE A fantastic day. There are not many events you're invited to that involve the whole family.
Gary Lineker keeps wicket as Guscott bats in a charity cricket match held by Michael Parkinson at Bray in August 1995.

passenger request: **Don't make flying on business such hard work**

Delta BusinessElite®:

on-line booking (easier to book)
telephone check-in* (easier to check-in)
executive lounges (easier to unwind in)
over 230 onward connections with Delta (easier to get to where you're going)

▲ **Delta**

fly more relaxed

See your travel agent or call 0800 414 767

delta-air.com

*Passengers with hand luggage only

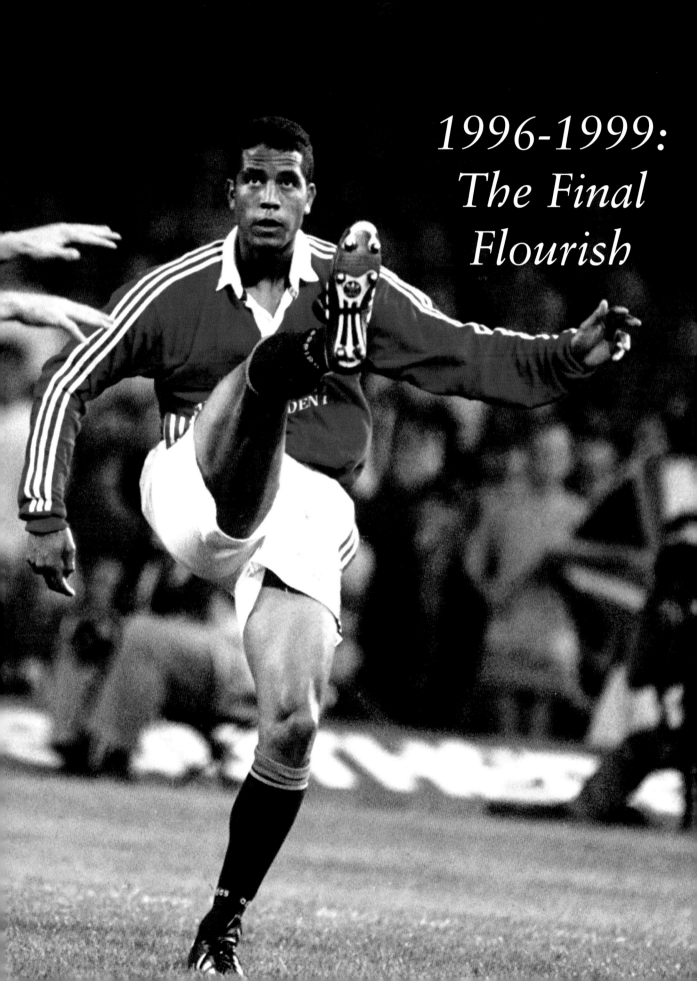

1996-1999:
The Final
Flourish

LEFT *A determined Jeremy Guscott on the charge in the Wakefield v Bath clash in February 1996. The hugely successful Bath club were on course for their sixth league championship in nine years, their third cup in a row (and tenth overall) and their fourth double. Once again, they swept the board.*

BELOW LEFT *I'd been filming* Body Heat *in Cape Town. I was training with Sally Gunnell and I pulled a muscle in my thigh. I came back and played in this match, and basically came back too early. But I had to play to prove my fitness because I couldn't have come back and gone straight into the cup final. In the last three or four minutes of this match, I made a break and was running down the touch line, and it just went again. That was the end of that – nice to win the league but a disappointment not to play in the cup final.*

Guscott in action for Bath in their crucial 1995-96 Courage League match against Sale on a tense final Saturday of the campaign. Bath were 32-12 up at half-time, but Sale recovered to gain a 38-38 draw. Yet Bath duly lifted the title because their title rivals, Leicester, came unstuck against Harlequins at Welford Road. The injury that Jeremy picked up in this match ruled him out of the Pilkington Cup final, in which Bath beat Leicester 16-15 through a controversial penalty try awarded in the last moments of normal time.

RIGHT *Guscott clutches the Courage League trophy after the 27 April match against Sale.*

LEFT I love golf and I love this event. It's very well organised and you get to play with some super players. I think over the years I've played with Montgomerie, Westwood, Clarke, Ballesteros, Woosnam, McNulty, and had some great days. When I first started playing, it was played at St Mellion. This one was played at the Oxfordshire and now it's played at the Belfry. But it's just a fantastic day out, playing a sport you love, and playing with some superstars. I don't play a great deal of pro-am, but I play the Benson and Hedges every year and I recently played in the 2000 Welsh Open pro-am, which was good fun.

Guscott plays from a bunker at the Oxfordshire during the pro-am competition at the 1996 Benson and Hedges International Open.

RIGHT AND BELOW The Welsh full back, Justin Thomas, went to kick, but I charged it down and just had to run 15 yards to get to it. Will was the nearest person there, and that was our little celebration for scoring the try. *England won this encounter 21-15. Played at Twickenham on 3 February, it was the second leg of their 1996 Five Nations; they had gone down 15-12 in Paris a fortnight earlier. Besides the Guscott score, this England v Wales game was notable as Robert Howley's international debut, on which he scored, and the occasion of Rory Underwood's 50th England try. England went on to beat Scotland 18-9 at Murrayfield and Ireland 28-15 at Twickenham to win the Triple Crown and take the championship on points difference ahead of Scotland.*

REACH FOR THE BEST

It's rare to find a recruitment consultancy who tackle personnel requirements with such tenacity and unfailing dedication. An unrivalled approach that has enabled Pertemps to remain unchallenged at the top of the league as the UK's leading independent recruitment consultancy.

As market leaders, we have developed our reputation not just by "filling positions" but by adding value to our client portfolio, a philosophy which is reflected in the diverse range of leading blue-chip companies that currently utilise our services.

Operating in three service divisions: commercial and professional, industrial and driving and technical and executive, our fully integrated service ensures that we are able to deliver quality personnel with the right skills, in the right place at the right time.

So, if you are seeking to win the competition for business, make sure that you retain the competition for talent by choosing Pertemps, Britain's most successful independent recruitment consultancy.

PERTEMPS
recruitment partnership

HEAD OFFICE:
Meriden Hall, Main Road, Meriden,
Warwickshire CV7 7PT.
Tel: 01676 525000 Fax: 01676 525009
Email: info@pertemps.co.uk
Web Site: www.pertemps.co.uk

1999

It all started when a magazine called *Bath City Life* got me to wear some clothing from a couple of different stores in Bath. Apart from that article, *Rugby Special* did a piece, and from there everybody thought I was a model. I did some modelling for other people, including Littlewoods and Cotton Traders, but I never took it seriously because I couldn't do it seriously. Rugby was what I was into.

LEFT *Modelling in Bath in 1989.*

BELOW LEFT *A summerwear assignment in 1993.*

BELOW *A promotional modelling session for Dickens and Jones in association with GQ.*

ABOVE The European Cup's a great addition to northern hemisphre rugby – something that everybody embraces and everybody loves.
Guscott shows the ball during the Bath v Dax European Cup clash in 1996-97, the first season in which English clubs participated. Bath won this match 25-16, but came second on points difference in their group behind the French club.

ABOVE LEFT *The 1996-97 competition also saw the first Scottish representation in the European Cup. Bath shared their group with Edinburgh, whom they defeated 55-26 in this match. Bath's run in the competition was eventually cut short by a 22-19 quarter-final defeat away at Cardiff.*

LEFT *Courage League action from the 1996-97 season, as Guscott takes out French flanker Laurent Cabannes of NEC Harlequins. Bath were runners-up that season, while Quins were third.*

ABOVE RIGHT *Further league action, Guscott this time launching an attack against Wasps while shadowed by Chris Sheasby. Wasps were the champions in what was the final season of the Courage Leagues, sponsorship passing to Allied Dunbar for the following season.*

RIGHT I think poor old Leicester – not that it should ever be poor old Leicester – had had a backlog of fixtures and we played them after they'd played a couple of games in close succession. They came to the Rec and we were on fire – we just tore them apart, basically. The try I scored in that match, I think, was a kick ahead and a race for the ball with Austin Healey, which I managed to win – which was quite nice!
Guscott takes on Leicester's World Cup winning South African fly half, Joel Stransky, during Bath's 47-9 drubbing of the Tigers in April 1997. This heavy league victory was sweet revenge for Bath, since Leicester, the eventual Pilkington Cup winners that year, had eliminated them from the competition in the sixth round.

LEFT I think we did well. It shows our durability. Throughout that centre partnership, I'm sure there were times, even though Will was captain, when people were asking why he should be playing, and at other times should I be playing. But it didn't work too badly, and I certainly enjoyed my time alongside Will.
Guscott with Will Carling during the national anthem before the England v Argentina match at Twickenham on 14 December 1996, the occasion of their 44th game as centre partners.

BELOW *Action from the match, which England won 20-18 through a try by Jason Leonard and five Mike Catt penalties to six penalties by Gonzalo Quesada. Here the Pumas' full back, Ezequiel Jurado, jumps to take a high ball, challenged by Guscott and Simon Shaw.*

ABOVE *Guscott steps around Field, the Ireland centre, during England's 46-6 triumph in Dublin, in which he appeared as a 76th-minute replacement for Will Carling.*

LEFT That season, I wasn't first choice. I came on against Ireland and against Wales. During the latter, I was on for the whole of the second half, playing, I felt, pretty well. On one occasion, I was breaking out and I thought I'd got away from Jonathan Davies, but even at that ripe old age he managed to tap-tackle me and sent me flying, nose ploughing into the Arms Park turf – which he never lets me forget.

Davies can only watch this time, as Guscott takes on Wayne Proctor. Guscott was introduced as replacement for John Sleightholme at the interval. Rothmans Rugby Union Yearbook 1997-98 *described what ensued, 'On an afternoon dedicated to farewells it was the unscripted arrival of an old favourite which made the headlines. Jeremy Guscott upstaged everything: the last match at the [Arms Park] stadium itself, and the last outings for Jonathan Davies, Rob Andrew and Will Carling... Guscott transformed the scoreboard and mood. He brought colour and excitement to a drab canvas. First he made a beautiful contribution to Stimpson's try... holding the defence with his swaying balanced run like a snake charmer toying with his pet. Then he did the same again for England's third try, fixing Thomas and then gliding past Williams before slipping the ball away to Hill from the midst of a massed tackle with the ease of a pickpocket filching a wallet away to his mates.'*

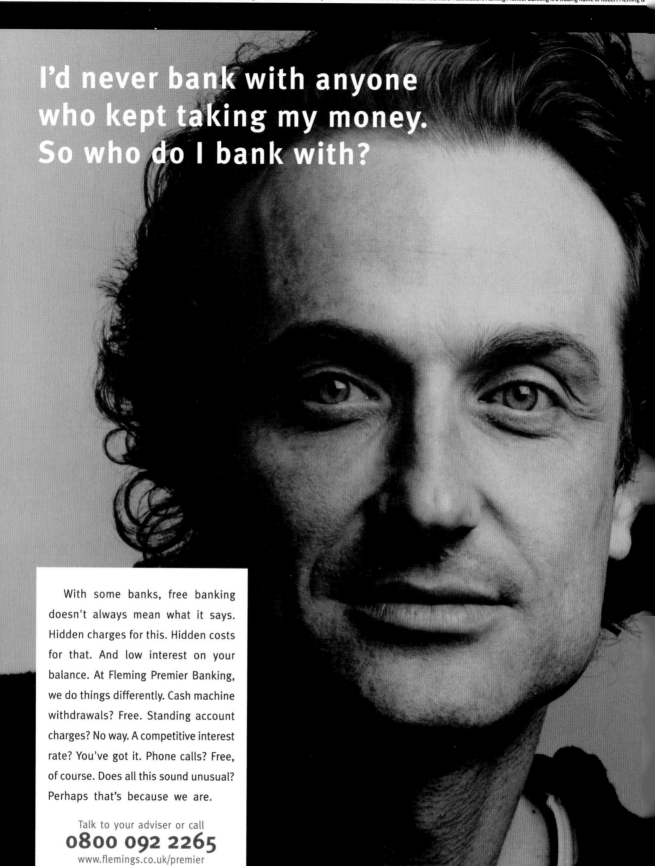

I'd never bank with anyone who kept taking my money. So who do I bank with?

With some banks, free banking doesn't always mean what it says. Hidden charges for this. Hidden costs for that. And low interest on your balance. At Fleming Premier Banking, we do things differently. Cash machine withdrawals? Free. Standing account charges? No way. A competitive interest rate? You've got it. Phone calls? Free, of course. Does all this sound unusual? Perhaps that's because we are.

Talk to your adviser or call

0800 092 2265

www.flemings.co.uk/premier

FLEMING
Premier Banking

2496/057

LEFT *The photocall for the 1997 British Lions tour of South Africa.*

BELOW I'd had to wait for my first match until the second game on the tours of 1989 and 1993. But this was the first game of the South Africa tour. A bit nerve-racking, but it was nice to start off with a win and score a couple of tries.

Guscott cuts inside Hennie le Roux on his way to scoring the first Lions try against an Eastern Province Invitational XV at Port Elizabeth on 24 May. The Lions ran out winners by 39 points to 11.

LEFT An old pro's way of getting out of training – 'Oh, I feel a bit tight. I need a bit of a rest.'
On the Lions physio couch.

BELOW I think the whole tour party felt up against it because I think we left with not too much support in terms of how successful the trip was going to be. I'd always believed that we could give a very good account of ourselves and push South Africa all the way. I don't think too many people outside the squad believed that. To win the 1st Test was great. There was some good rugby played there, and the boys defended so well.
Guscott breaks with Gregor Townsend in support during the 1st Test at Cape Town, which the Lions won 25-16.

ABOVE RIGHT *Guscott gets attention from Henry Honiball and Ruben Kruger during the 2nd Test at Durban. Lawrence Dallaglio arrives as back-up.*

RIGHT *Guscott and Neil Jenkins bring South Africa's Andre Joubert to a standstill in the 2nd Test. Joubert scored one of his side's three tries at Durban.*

ABOVE AND LEFT I'm sure any South African who watched the 2nd Test can't believe that they lost, because they scored all the tries and took a lot of possession. But when we had to defend, we defended so well. I just felt that they believed they were going to win, and thought that we were going to roll over. But their discipline was so bad that they kept giving Neil Jenkins the opportunities, and that guy just doesn't miss. Then the chance came to me, after a couple of drives from the boys, and I think the only person outside me was Austin Healey, and there was no way I was going to give him the ball, because we wouldn't have heard the last of it. It was just right time, right place, right person, and over it went. The first person to arrive was Gibbsy, who I've got so much respect for. He had a massive tour; was man of the tour. My first thoughts after the game were 'What if I'd missed?' I don't know why I thought that because it's such a negative thought, which I don't generally have. But it was such a massive moment. It must be like winning the lottery. You get five straight numbers and the next number comes out and it's yours as well and you've won it. And you think 'Well, what would have happened if it wasn't mine?' – it was just a weird sensation. *Not even Henry Honiball at full stretch can stop the Guscott dropped goal that took the score from 15-15 to 18-15 to bring a Lions victory in the 2nd Test. Scott Gibbs is first on the scene to congratulate his centre partner.*

RIGHT McGeechan was one of those blokes who could talk to a threequarter as he could to a forward and get the same kind of response and respect. And he had the credibility. He's just a really nice guy. Easy to get along with.

A delighted Guscott with an equally delighted Ian McGeechan, the Lions coach, after the final whistle had gone in the 2nd Test at Durban. McGeechan and Guscott collaborated on three Lions tours – to Australia in 1989, to New Zealand in 1993 and to South Africa in 1997.

BELOW *Guscott reminds anybody who is watching that the series score stands at 2-0 to the Lions. With him are Lions skipper Martin Johnson (centre) and Neil Jenkins, whose five penalties kept the Lions in the game.*

OFFICIAL
BEER
ENGLAND
RUGBY

www.smoothlydoesit.co.uk

LEFT Me and Saskia meeting for the first time. She was by then about three weeks old and it was great to see her. It was great to see all the girls – Imogen, Holly, Jayne. You're always glad to get home, but I was especially glad on that occasion because I'd not seen my new daughter. I'd broken my arm in the last game, and it took all that pain away.

Guscott meets his newborn daughter Saskia at the airport. After the euphoria of the 2nd Test, an exhausted Lions side went down 35-16 against South Africa in the 3rd Test, at Ellis Park, Johannesburg. But the series was in the bag. Guscott broke a bone in his arm during the 3rd Test, and was replaced for the second half by Allan Bateman.

BELOW It was a great achievement by everybody – it just so happens that I was the person who dropped the goal, and people say that won the series. Well, I suppose it brought the final points to win it, but it was a hard slog. I always think the Lions is a great experience, with great tradition. To be part of a squad that wins in South Africa, which some say is the hardest place to win a series, is no mean achievement. It's just brilliant.
With Martin Johnson and the spoils of victory.

LEFT *Body Heat* was quite an experience, and working with Mike Smith was an experience in itself. The guy was so professional. I think in the two series I saw Mike trip up once, and that was it, whereas Sally Gunnell and myself were just all over the place. It was nerve-racking but good fun.

Guscott presented the series Body Heat *with Olympic hurdler Sally Gunnell and television personality Mike Smith. Teams of two competed over a range of physical tests. The 1995 final took place in Atlanta, Georgia, and Guscott is pictured with the cheerleaders of the Atlanta Falcons football team.*

TOP LEFT *Although his television work has usually been sport or fitness orientated, in 1996, Guscott presented a six-part BBC2 documentary series called* Top Score, *which introduced children to the world of opera.*

ABOVE LEFT AND ABOVE A pretty tough schedule. It takes four hours to film and from that you get one hour's television. It was great experience to work with Ulrika. She pretty much nursemaided me through it. It was such a big programme with such a huge profile that to walk out into that environment in front of 7,000 people was mega. I've been lucky. I've had some huge experiences and that would be one of them.

In 1997, Guscott fronted Gladiators *with Ulrika Jonsson.*

ABOVE RIGHT Before *Body Heat* I did a programme for HTV called *Let's Go*, with Jill Impey, the weather presenter for HTV. It was about the HTV region and what was on and where to go to find it.

Guscott with Let's Go *co-presenter Jill Impey in 1992.*

RIGHT *In 1999, Guscott collaborated again with Sally Gunnell in the three-programme Channel 4 sports series* Peak Performance, *which dealt with diet, fitness and training, and sports injuries.*

GROVE INDUSTRIES LIMITED

Grove Industries Limited

congratulate Jeremy Guscott on his

outstanding contribution to Rugby Football

and wish him every success for the future

Birmingham Road, Stratford upon Avon CV37 0AS

LEFT AND BELOW A magic moment for the club and for everybody involved. You can't get much bigger for your club, really – they are the guys that you've sweated with for days and weeks and months, and you play in a cup final of which the outcome is that you're the best club in Europe. There were a number of occasions during that match when we didn't think we were going to win, and we came through. You've just got to look at the way the side reacted at the final whistle, when everybody just sprinted off, arms raised aloft. It was just a mega, mega day.

Bath beat Brive 19-18 in Bordeaux on 31 January 1998 to become the first English club to win the European Cup. Jon Callard scored all Bath's points, including a try; Brive replied with five penalties from Christophe Lamaison and an Alain Penaud dropped goal.

ABOVE *Guscott tries to hand off Thomas Castaignède during England's 24-17 defeat against eventual 1998 Grand Slam winners France in Paris. Guscott was recalled for this game having missed the matches against the touring southern hemisphere sides because of injury.*

LEFT I nearly scored a try against Wales, but Scott Gibbs stopped me right on the line. There are some things he will do and there are some things he won't – he'll give me a try-scoring pass, but he won't let me score against him. Throughout your career you see people lead the team out, and it was nice to lead England out against Wales at Twickenham, and then we stuffed them. A good way to celebrate my 50th cap.
A little celebration after a training session prior to winning his 50th England cap at Twickenham on 21 February 1998. England beat Wales that day by 60 points to 26, registering a record score for the championship and equalling their own record score in Tests.

ABOVE RIGHT *Trying to move the ball before the tackle comes in against Ireland. England won this encounter 35-17 to lift their fourth successive Triple Crown.*

RIGHT *Guscott bursts through on his way to one of his four tries in England's 110-0 win over the Netherlands in the 1999 World Cup qualifier in November1998.*

65% OF THE MARKET HAS ALREADY SWITCHED.*

ARE YOU IN OR OUT?

With its superior retention and innovative, lightweight design, Fast Twist™ by Trisport™ is the new standard in cleat insert technology. One simple quarter-turn locks cleats into place, so they're easy to install and replace. That's why FootJoy,® Dexter,® Lady Fairway,™ Adidas,® Bite,™ Wilson®† and a growing number of shoe manufacturers have already switched. And why you should, too.
Fast Twist. Easy In. Easy Out.

Cleat Insert System

RIGHT AND BELOW A disappointing result because we played well, and to lose it was a bit of a 'gutter'. For them, that's the sign of a good side – if you can play pretty well, and the other side play better, but you still win. *Guscott scores the only try of the game in the Cook Cup match between England and Australia at Twickenham on 28 November 1998. Australia shaded this game 12-11.*

FOLLOWING PAGES We sorted it out the following week when we beat South Africa. They were going for the world record of consecutive Test victories, and we managed to stop them. They were pretty tired from all their travelling and the games they'd played. Still, South Africans don't like getting beaten at any time. And we played some great rugby. It was one of the best atmospheres Twickenham has had since the redevelopment – and a massive night of celebration. *Guscott about to score in England's 13-7 win over South Africa at Twickenham on 5 December 1998.*

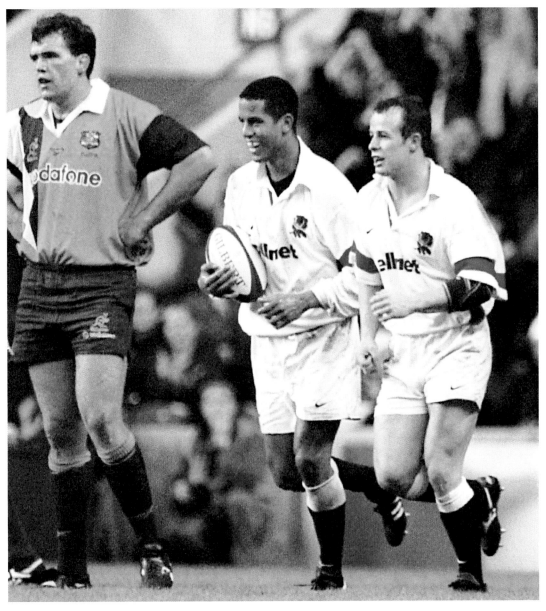

I enjoyed the 1998-99 season. I captained the Bath side a couple of times, which was a great honour, having been born and bred in the city. There were some moments at the Rec that season which were some of my best times.

LEFT *Touching down for Bath against Wasps in September 1998. Bath finished sixth in the Allied Dunbar Premiership that season, one place below Wasps, both sides qualifying for European rugby in 1999-2000. Bath's qualification hinged on their final match against London Scottish, whom they crushed in a 12-try display, with Guscott scoring four of them. London Scottish were about to disappear, at least temporarily, from the big time, having been taken over by London Irish.*

RIGHT *Leading out Bath at the Rec, accompanied by the mascot, for the match against Harlequins in May 1999.*

BELOW *About to score again for Bath, this time against Richmond, despite Craig Quinnell's best efforts. Richmond, also taken over by London Irish, were another famous name to drop out of the professional ranks for the foreseeable future at the end of the 1998-99 season.*

We're right behind you too.

save & prosper

part of Fleming Asset Management

ABOVE *Guscott takes on Scotland's Glenn Metcalfe during England's 24-21 triumph in the 1999 Calcutta Cup encounter at Twickenham.*

RIGHT *Prop Paul Wallace closes Guscott down in Dublin. England won this game 27-15 to keep their unbeaten record intact going into the third leg of the championship.*

FAR RIGHT This looks a lot worse that it was, although I did lose the ball. It was a move that we normally did with Will Greenwood, but we used me instead, and I just ran into a French brick wall.
Guscott comes up against solid French defence during the England v France clash at Twickenham. England secured victory 21-10 – seven Jonny Wilkinson penalties to a Franck Comba try and two successful kicks (one penalty, one conversion) by Thomas Castaignède. This was Guscott's final championship appearance, injury ruling him out of the 32-31 defeat to Wales at Wembley, in which England's Grand Slam hopes were killed off by Scott Gibbs with seconds of the campaign left to run, leaving Scotland as the winners of the last Five Nations Championship.

ABOVE This was our only warm-up game on the 1999 summer tour of Australia. It wasn't the full Queensland side – they had a lot of players in camp getting ready for the World Cup. The match was at Ballymore, which it was nice to revisit.
Guscott breaks past Nathan Williams and Damian Smith to score for England v Queensland in June 1999.

LEFT Tim's a great guy and a great player. I played with him once for a World XV against New Zealand; it was nice to have that experience. I think the only thing new about this game was our shirts. As usual they beat us. But it was nice to play in the Olympic stadium. Rightly or wrongly, I think the biggest buzz I got was walking on the track thinking that great athletes were going to be running finals there in just over a year's time.
Guscott held by Tim Horan during the Australia v England Centenary Test in Sydney on 26 June 1999, which the Wallabies won 22-15.

ABOVE RIGHT I scored the try that took it over 100, which is a nice memory. We've got the US player Dan Lyle at Bath, and if he pipes up in training we just say, 'Shut up. What are you talking about? We beat you by 100 points', which is a drastic measure, but when you need someone to pipe down...
England defeat the USA 106-8 in the World Cup warm-up match at Twickenham in August 1999.

RIGHT *Action from England's 36-11 win in the warm-up match against Canada at Twickenham later that month.*

LEFT *Held up against Italy in England's first group match of the 1999 World Cup. England won 67-7 – eight tries and 11 Jonny Wilkinson kicks (five penalties and six conversions) to a try and conversion by Diego Dominguez. Guscott was not originally selected for this game, but came on as a replacement. He was, however, in the starting line-up for England's second game, against New Zealand, which the All Blacks won 30-16 to condemn England to a quarter-final play-off to qualify for the quarter-finals proper.*

BELOW LEFT AND RIGHT My last run and my last try. That was when I knew it was pretty much over – the groin had sort of torn up by then. It was a run that was quite enjoyable, although I would have preferred it if it hadn't been so far. But that was it.
Guscott runs virtually the length of the field to touch down in England's final group match of the 1999 World Cup, the 101-10 defeat of Tonga, which proved to be his last match in an England shirt.

BELOW I suppose it seemed that I could have left it until after the World Cup, but it was on my mind and I didn't want to go through the rest of the tournament knowing that was what I was going to say at the end of it. I'd already discussed it with the various parties, and that was that – the end of my international career. I'm not unhappy about it. I can sit down and watch England play now, and I'm quite happy to watch and don't feel the urge to play.
Guscott announces his retirement from international rugby in Paris on 21 October 1999.

LEFT *The Bath photocall for 1999-2000. Although retired from the international game, Guscott remained a club player with Bath, although injury prevented him from appearing in the 1999-2000 season.*

BELOW *Being presented with an RFU Outstanding Achievement Award by Clive Woodward at the RFU Annual Charity Awards Dinner in May 2000. Guscott's contribution to English rugby was further acknowledged in HM the Queen's Birthday Honours list for 2000, in which Jeremy received an MBE.*

For the Record

Name: Jeremy Clayton Guscott **Born:** 7 July 1965 **Height:** 6ft 1in **Weight:** 13st 10lb

Bath
Club debut: v Waterloo 1984-85 **League debut:** *v Moseley 1987-88*
RFU Cup – **Winner's medals:** 6 (1985 (*rep*), 87 (*rep*), 89, 90, 92, 95)
League – **Winner's medals:** 6 (1989, 91, 92, 93, 94, 96)

England
International debut: v Romania 1989 *Five Nations debut:* v Ireland 1990
1989: Ro, Fi; **1990:** Ir, Wa, Fr, Sc, Ar; **1991:** Wa, Sc, Ir, Fr, Fi, Au, RWC (NZ, It, Fr, Sc, Au); **1992:** Sc, Ir, Fr, Wa, Ca, SA; **1993:** Fr, Wa, Sc, Ir; **1994:** Ro, Ca; **1995:** Ir, Fr, Wa, Sc, RWC (Ar, It, Au, NZ, Fr), SA, W Sam; **1996:** Fr, Wa, Sc, Ir; **1997:** Ir (*rep*), Wa (*rep*); **1998:** Fr, Wa, Sc, Ir, Ho, It, Au, SA; **1999:** Sc, Ir, Fr, Au, USA, Ca, RWC (It (*rep*), NZ, To)
Caps: 65 **Points:** 143 **Tries:** 30 **Dropped Goals:** 2
Grand Slams: 1991, 92, 95; **Triple Crowns:** 1991, 92, 95, 96, 97, 98

British Lions
1989: Au (2nd and 3rd Tests); **1993:** NZ (1st, 2nd, 3rd); **1997:** SA (1st, 2nd, 3rd)

Also played two Tests for a World XV against New Zealand to celebrate the centenary of the NZRU in April 1992, represented the Four Home Unions against a Rest of Europe XV in 1990 and played several times for the Barbarians

League Record		
Season	*Apps*	*Tries*
1987-88	10	1
1988-89	8	10
1989-90	9	4
1990-91	11	5
1991-92	7	1
1992-93	10	3
1993-94	2	2
1994-95	8	1
1995-96	14	9
1996-97	19	12
1997-98	11	5
1998-99	19	14
Total:	128	67

Has also kicked eight conversions and dropped a goal in League matches

All-time leading try scorers in top division of league rugby

Tries	Player
67	Jeremy Guscott
63	Daren O'Leary
56	Rory Underwood
54	Adedayo Adebayo

League Highlights

1987-88: scores first league try, v Sale at Heywood Road; he also kicked five conversions in the match as he split the kicking duties with John Palmer.

1988-89: scores first hat-trick, v Moseley away on 12 November 1988; topped the Courage Division One try-scoring list with a new record total of 10.

1989-90: scores four tries in a Courage League match for the first time as Bath thrash Bedford 76-0 on 13 January 1990.

1995-96: scores hat-trick as Bath beat Bristol 52-9 on 14 October 1995.

1996-97: breaks Tony Swift's record of 43 tries with a try against Saracens on 14 January 1997.

1998-99: scores four tries for the second time, in the final game of the season at home to London Scottish on 15 May 1999; ends season with a new best of 14 tries from 19 starts.

PICTURE ACKNOWLEDGEMENTS

The Publishers are grateful to the following for their permission to use the photographs on the pages listed: (t=top, b=bottom, m=middle, r=right, l=left)

Allsport UK: 16, 22b, 25all, 27t, 29t&b, 30t, 31t&b, 34-35, 37b, 38t&b, 39t, 43, 45t, 47t&b, 52t&b, 53t&b, 55t&b, 56t&b, 59t&b, 60t&b, 61t&b, 65b, 68t&m, 69t, 70-71, 73t, 75t, 76, 77, 78l, 79t&b, 80b, 81b, 83, 84, 86b, 87t&b, 88b, 91br, 92tl, 93b, 94t, 98t&b, 101t&b, 103t&b, 107t, 108t&b, 109t, 111t, 118t&b, 120b, 121t, 123b, 125b, 126, 128
Colorsport: 21t, 23b, 26b, 27b, 30b, 45b, 50t&b, 51t&b, 63b, 66-67, 68b, 69b, 75b, 80t, 81t, 88-90, 92tr, 95t&b, 97t, 99b, 100t&b, 112-113, 120t, 122b
SpedeGrafix 99: 8, 32-33, 39b, 40-41, 57t&b, 62, 65t, 72t, 78r, 86t, 92b, 93t, 97b, 99t, 107b, 109b, 111b, 114t&b, 115, 119, 121b, 122t, 123t, 125t
Bath Chronicle: 20t&b, 22-23t, 22b, 26t, 37t 44t&b, 48-49, 63t, 72b, 91t&bl, 105m
BBC Television: 104tl
Carlton UK Television: 104b
Daily Express: 73b
Glasshead Ltd/Channel 4: 105b
London Weekend Television: 104tr, 105t
Walcot Old Boys RFC: 19

The Publishers would also like to thank Stephen Jones and Maria Pedro for their editorial assistance in the captioning of the photographs.